T0114698

Me, Myself, and I
The Human Case of
Mistaken Identity Series

Me, Myself, and I
The Human Case of
Mistaken Identity Series

Book 1

Leda Mitrofanis

BALBOA.PRESS
A DIVISION OF HAY HOUSE

Balboa Press books may be ordered through booksellers or by contacting:

Balboa Press
A Division of Hay House
1663 Liberty Drive
Bloomington, IN 47403
www.balboapress.com
844-682-1282

Because of the dynamic nature of the Internet, any web addresses or
links contained in this book may have changed since publication and
may no longer be valid. The views expressed in this work are solely those
of the author and do not necessarily reflect the views of the publisher,
and the publisher hereby disclaims any responsibility for them.

The author of this book does not dispense medical advice or prescribe the use
of any technique as a form of treatment for physical, emotional, or medical
problems without the advice of a physician, either directly or indirectly. The
intent of the author is only to offer information of a general nature to help
you in your quest for emotional and spiritual well-being. In the event you use
any of the information in this book for yourself, which is your constitutional
right, the author and the publisher assume no responsibility for your actions.

Any people depicted in stock imagery provided by Getty Images are
models, and such images are being used for illustrative purposes only.
Certain stock imagery © Getty Images.

Print information available on the last page.

ISBN: 979-8-7652-4058-8 (sc)
ISBN: 979-8-7652-4060-1 (hc)
ISBN: 979-8-7652-4059-5 (e)

Library of Congress Control Number: 2023905732

Balboa Press rev. date: 03/30/2023

Dedication

This book is dedicated to my son, George,

for all the love and light, you brought into

my life and to everyone you touch.

and

to all of you who are searching for your identity.

Acknowledgements

Immeasurable thanks to my mentor Elaine DeGiorgio

and to my guide, Anthony

There are no words to express my love and gratitude.

Contents

Introduction

What it is like to be a child of identity theft? Let me tell you what that looks like and what it feels like. It's the ultimate and highest form of rejection. It's not being seen or heard, a pervasive sense of invisibility. It's realizing that not only does your presence not matter, but when it's noticed it's more of a hindrance than anything else. It's being de-valued in every which way possible – physically, emotionally, mentally, socially. It's being verbally abused, in the most subtle of ways and under the guise of "I love you, that's why I'm telling you the truth of how it is." It's being labeled, pigeon-holed, beaten down, diminished spiritually until you realize you are nothing. You finally come to believe that you have no inherent value, that your only value derives from pleasing others and being all things to all people so that you will be liked and approved of. You exist in a constant state of "I am not good enough." You trust yourself not at all, so you constantly look outside of yourself for validation and guidance. You constantly give your power away. But worst of all, you do not even realize this is all happening to you because it happens so slowly and most times so subtly as a plane flying just under the radar.

What do you feel like? Like you've been stolen…as if someone snatched you right out of your body slowly but surely, bit by bit, a piece here, a piece there. Your sense of self completely taken before you have a chance to recognize it, explore it, nourish it, and expand it yourself. None of this is done intentionally, of course, as in the case of our parents. They do the best they can with the knowledge they have at the time. They too most likely were also victims of some form of identity theft in their childhood and if they never became conscious of it, they merely repeated the patterns they experienced and learned from their own parents and bequeathed it onto their children. Hence, the children become an extension of their egos, and all the shortcomings they experienced now become passed down to the next generation. And so, the cycle continues, on repeat.

Identity theft starts with our parents in our nuclear family and then emanates outward like a sound wave to include our extended family, our teachers, caregivers, friends, the media, social media, and society at large, until we are all walking around searching for ourselves, looking for and trying to reclaim our own sense of self all the awhile hijacking and annihilating one another in the process.

So how do we bring this endless cycle to a halt? How do we solve our individual and humanity's identity crisis?

Everything that exists in our outer world begins within us first. As within, so without. Therefore, our work is to go within to identify who we are.

Me, Myself, and I is the first book in the series, The Human Case of Mistaken Identity.

This series is a culmination of experiences, lessons, emotions, studies, and sojourns into the unseen; partly exhausting, partly frustrating but mostly nourishing. It's a pushing and prodding, sometimes pulling, and at times a kick in the back side to rouse us into who we are. It's the human journey into our authentic identity. It's the way back home to ourselves and source. To get there has been humanity's greatest challenge both personally and collectively as we look to ease suffering, understand our challenges, and to find guidance and tools to help us. To live a life that is the fullest expression of ourselves requires the knowledge and alignment of our human identity along with the knowledge and integration of our spiritual identity.

Book One is the starting point of understanding our identities and how they integrate. As you move through the book, keep an open mind, and pause to integrate. As we explore the trinity that is our human make-up and discover our spiritual identity, the pieces of the puzzle will start to come together. To change our lives to the peace, harmony, unity, equanimity and love we desire we must first know who we are and why we're here.

<u>Note:</u> As you move through the text, you will find it concise, simple and to the point. Essentially, I believe in landing the plane and not circling the runway, which can keep us in a state of confusion. You will see I pose many questions and refrain from providing certain answers and detailed examples. The purpose of this is to have you thinking and going within to seek out your own answers, not mine or anyone else's.

Let's go.

CHAPTER 1

Identity Crisis

Part I

I suffered from an identity crisis my entire life and didn't even know it.

Actually... so do you... and so does about 99% of humanity.

I grew up in the borough of Queens in New York City to immigrant Greek and Cypriot parents. It's quite ironic, when I think about it now because Greeks are thought to be a culture in which a very strong sense of identity resides. There is a great pride instilled in those who are born within the Greek heritage. From birth that strong sense of the Greek identity is instilled; it's who you are – it's a cultural, moral, specific way of life that most Greeks adopt and adhere to. I remember when I lived in Greece in my late 20's- early 30's, I was never considered "Greek American" but "Greek", as Greek nationals were constantly correcting me. This strong sense of Greek identity was not a negative trait. It served its purpose when Greece had to fight and win its independence and then during WWII, when they battle cried their famous "No" to Nazi Germany spawning Winston Churchills' famous quote: "Greeks don't fight like heroes, heroes fight like Greeks." It was that strong an identity, historically forged deep within the ethnic lineage.

When I was a child in the early 70's, I attended public school till 3pm and then sent to Greek afternoon school, it was a mix of language, culture, history, and dance all liberally peppered with a huge dose of nationalism. Growing up in New York City however, I never totally fed into the whole nationalistic aspect of the school. Not for any reason other than for some unknown purpose at that time, I was interested in and felt that in some way I was also connected to many other people and cultures in the world as well. I sensed, without consciously knowing it, that there was an underlying cord or thread that bound all humans on the planet. I might have been born Greek, but I felt I was much more than that. When I lived in Greece in my late 20's-early 30's, for a seven-year duration, I was still in my previous career as an Executive Producer of TV Commercials and my work took me to other countries, in addition to my own travels. These experiences allowed me to peer up close to many different cultures, to meet people of all nationalities and races, and to converse with them in meaningful ways. And each time, I came away with the same conclusion that "deep inside we are all the same." Interestingly enough, this was also my high school yearbook quote many years earlier. As part of the human identity, we all share the same emotions garnered from different yet similar experiences, we all eventually come to the same wisdom gleaned from many different stories. It's ultimately one play with many different characters, scenes, and acts.

As I became more and more aware of this, I became fascinated with the stories of all the different people I met. My listening afforded me the luxury of observing the common threads that ran through all of us. And ultimately that we all suffered from the same loss and separation, trying each of us in our own way to reclaim it: the loss and separation from our core identity; our essence. I realized that this fundamental teaching was clearly missing. How ironic that I was taught from birth all about my human identity but not that I was a spiritual being having a temporary physical existence of my choosing and my creation; for the purpose of remembering my true essence and thus expanding my own consciousness, that of those around me while simultaneously being a vital element of the collective human consciousness.

This truth changes everything.

Part II

I was raised in the Greek Orthodox Church and as a young child and teen I resonated closely with Jesus and Mother Mary. I will never forget one Holy Thursday service; I was about 11 years old. The 12 gospel readings of the crucifixion are read. After the sixth reading, the priest, altar boys, cantors begin a procession around the church of a huge cross bearing a crucified Jesus to which we all solemnly kneel while hymns are sung. I did not kneel but stood with bowed head. As the procession approached where I was sitting, I felt a sudden intense wave of tremendous sadness and grief and in those moments, I was transported back in time literally feeling that I had been present at the event thousands of years before. It was very real, exceptionally vivid, and very strongly felt…as if I was remembering a long stored away memory. It did not scare me. As children do, I just accepted and stayed with the feeling until it passed. There was no judgement and I never spoke of it. It wasn't until many years later in my late

40's that I had a dream, followed by a strong experience of the presence of Mother Mary, which prompted a past life regression which confirmed that I was in fact there. This happening, it turned out, was my initial nudge into where I was headed.

By the time I got to college, the church answers to my ever-growing questions of who we were, why we were here and what were we doing here were insufficient. I felt they were missing a key piece of vital importance although I could not articulate what. So, I began reading and researching other world religions only to feel that each one presented a piece of a larger puzzle. I didn't feel that any of them were able to encompass the truth I was searching for. Plus, they were all tainted with the economic, political, and social agenda's that I felt ran contrary and astray from the spiritual truths on which they were founded.

This is when I realized that my answers would not come from the outer world or outside of myself but from within. This was not an outward search but an inward one. I sensed that there was a whole component of myself that

I had yet to discover. On some level we all know this, it is the core of who we are after all, but we have forgotten and come to this conscious remembering at some point in our lives through the many experiences we have chosen to have - or to say it another way; from life itself.

Thus, my journey took a pivotal and significant turn when I embarked on the search for my answers from within. In the 15 year span that followed; I read, questioned, researched, studied, got degrees, wrote in my journal, cried, analyzed, examined, cried some more, wrote some more, attended more seminars and classes, made new friends, let go of old friends, married, divorced, married and divorced again, had a child, changed careers thrice, explored and dappled in many different alternative spiritual modalities until I stripped away all of my human ego story complete with its labels, attached beliefs, self-judgments, stereotyping and disconnectedness. It was not easy, nor for the faint of heart. It was hard and at times very hard. I won't be going into all my experiences in this book, there is so much it is a story for another time. What is important is that each time I learned to ask myself, what is this experience helping me to remember about who I am, why I am here and what I am being that I have forgotten? I learned to look at every experience, every interaction as a teaching and a signpost from the universe (and myself – but more on that later) guiding me to remember my core identity and the purpose for which I came.

Towards the end of this 15 year span I clearly saw that humanity was collectively suffering from what I call "a case of mistaken identity". 15 years earlier, when I first moved back from Europe and left my first career behind me with it, I met a woman who was a hands-on healer. At the time I suffered from low back pain, and I was intrigued by the whole concept and if she could truly help. After my session she disclosed that she was a channel and that Mother Mary had come through to her during my session. I thought, there it is again. She asked me if I could do anything in this lifetime, without any restrictions, what would I truly want to do. Without missing a beat, I responded I would change the world by teaching humanity, especially the young generation, about who they truly are. I had no idea where this came from. It was out of my mouth before my brain had a chance to get into gear. I knew nothing at the time of all the things I am writing about in this book! I was at the beginning...but I left with a distant thought that my life was on a specific trajectory of which I had yet to be aware of. And that trajectory, involved correcting humanity's understanding of their identity, specifically beginning with the age from which we begin to forget, those tender pre-adolescent years and on into young adulthood.

Moving forward, I reflected constantly on this statement I blurted out...what was I talking about? How could I affect shift in anything on such a scale? Who did I think I was? And why the youth? Round and round I went. But eventually my false ego mind became more silenced, and I was able to hear my inner voice. What emerged was more of: I am going to teach and offer what I was never taught to help others navigate their way into and through the world without it hijacking and annihilating their core sense of self. I would help them to understand their core root, so they may learn to use it as their guiding foundation for whenever they felt lost, confused, disillusioned, desperate, hurt, or despondent. They would know where to turn for healing and direction. I would lead them to understand that this "core essence" is their origin and from there everything else stems. I would teach them that this identity is beyond their human identity of ethnicity, culture, race, religion and existence. It is their spiritual identity.

There is a saying that reads the wounded becomes the healer. In having my own sense of self taken away from me at a very young age and thereafter, (again a story for another time) I had become very adept in giving myself away, in being all things to all those around me who needed something all the while neglecting my own needs and thus never giving fertile ground for the blossoming of my own self. I became who I was told I was, and I did this very well to my own detriment. Over the years, this caused me so much pain, because there is no pain greater than that of the separation from self, from our core essence. From there all other separation stems.

When I gave birth to my son, I instinctively and silently vowed to myself that I would raise him with a sense of his true spiritual identity. I knew by this point that this would be the most important gift I could give him – to give him back to himself and not to take away who he is to fill any personal agenda I might have or have him serve as an extension of my ego. I knew that this gift, this knowledge, this teaching of never letting him forget who he was would alter the direction of his life. It would shift the perspective from which he operated as an adult; affect every decision, harness his ever-expanding consciousness, his compassion and empathy, his sense of equanimity and harmony. It would always allow him to speak his truth and stay in peace. But most importantly it would allow him to move in this world without fear.

This too was a process, but as it turned out a joyous one although daunting. I learned as much from raising my son in this manner, as he learned from me. In giving him a sense of himself I was able to reclaim my own sense of self. It was the silver lining I did not expect. As a single mom I faced many challenges, but this was my greatest. Soon I found I began expanding to my son's friends and before I knew it, kids began coming to me with all sorts of questions and challenges they faced looking for some way to help them cope and make sense of life. This then led to fellow parents, friends and colleagues who began looking for insight. Consequently, and simultaneously my work began to take shape and my vision birthed itself.

Through my work I saw that each of us is instinctively aware of our inner self. The question is to what degree. As young children we are more aware and live this out with our spontaneity, free-spiritedness, authenticity, joy for the mere sake of being, but living in the human world it is knocked out of us with each passing year, eventually becoming a suppressed memory. We are told to stop living in fantasy land or the world of the woo-hoo and to live "in reality". The question is whose reality? In every moment we are making choices that define who we are. Our behaviors stem from these choices and these choices stem from our beliefs. What are we taught to believe? What are we choosing to believe? I knew then, that for our human condition to change we had to return to the beginning, to the point where we begin to forget and alter our social conditioning.

So, let's look at the current state of our human identity.

CHAPTER 2

Our Changing World

Our world and society are ever evolving and changing. Our daily lives have shifted dramatically from where we were 50 years ago with the most substantial and noticeable difference in technology. The rate of its expansion and upgrading has changed and re-shaped how we live, work and play. It's affected the way we communicate (write/speak), how we socialize, how we teach in our schools, our medical care, how we do business across all industries and predominantly how our younger generation is molded. There are many pros and cons which is not the focus here but rather an observation of what these changes are, the effect of them on society and its trajectory.

The world of instant communication and an unbridled global access to information, whether personal or professional, has resulted in unprecedented communication overload. Humanity scrambles to keep up with the daily political, social, and cultural news. Companies and various professions have evolved to a 24hr on-call expectation of email response in addition to the increase of continuing education required for new and upgraded software programs and apps. And lastly, let's not forget the specific personal interests of everyone that keeps us scrolling. The point? We are glued to one type of screen or another most of the day. What is the outcome and trajectory of this type of constant communication overload? Is it burnout to an unparalleled degree? Anger? Frustration? Anxiety? Mental disturbance and processing exhaustion? Endless competition? Elimination of any non-tech downtime?

In the realm of technology outreach, social media is its most precarious tool. While opening the connection and sharing of our lives with friends and relatives in other countries, sourcing new clients for our businesses and seeing places and events as if in our own backyard its opposing effect has been a 24/7 attention rate that effects our sleep cycles, our vision, our body image, our belief and behavior systems and our very sense of self.

As the ultimate marketing tool of self-branding, suddenly we are in a constant state of comparison and competition with everyone else in every aspect of our existence. Suddenly those feelings of "not being good enough" or feelings of "unworthiness" become magnified a thousand-fold. Suddenly negative and hurtful opinions are on the rise due to the anonymity provided. Suddenly fear and stress are part of our daily existence because of FOMO (Fear of Missing Out). Suddenly we are experiencing feelings of self -defeat, insecurity, isolation, endless competition resulting in a pressure to over-achieve and excel in well...everything...if that was even possible. Suddenly and over time we begin to shrink back from everything we knew to be true about ourselves and most importantly, suddenly we give our power away to everyone and everything outside of ourselves so we can feel valued and significant. And most detrimental of all we start to create a digital persona and existence that we do not have or live so we can attain this feeling.

In this world of constant chatter and incessant distraction we're suddenly beginning to question who we are. This endless hamster wheel leaves no room for innate creativity and personal growth. It leaves no room for the cultivation of stillness, of downtime, and for the art of doing nothing at all. The art of dwelling in a complete state of *being* as opposed to *doing*. If you spend any time with young children, you will see a change. Their innate imagination has been pushed aside in favor of constant exterior stimulation. They are learning to look outside of themselves as opposed to sourcing from within. They organically reach within but what chance does the new generation have when we put a device in their hands from early infancy to keep them distracted so we can go about our lives while ironically trying to keep up ourselves? Where does humanity go from here?

When the outside world is so noisy, we hear our inner voice less and less causing a slow but steady disconnection from our inner wisdom, inner compass, and our sense of self.

Additionally, growing up in an achievement-oriented world has fostered competition to an unparalleled scale. The internet and TV are full of competition shows in one form or another cultivating this need to prove we have value by being better than someone else. The push to excel in all areas has left humanity emotionally and mentally exhausted. This drive to over-achieve begins from when we are born with parents pushing their children to cover milestones that are simply not developmentally appropriate or feasible. In favor of having their child stand out parents push and train them to speak in full words starting at 3 mos. Kindergarteners are given written math assessments with directionals when they can't even read. As an educator I've seen this first-hand, as well as so many well-intentioned parents running around giving their children all sorts of lessons in all areas for the purpose of having a leg up to compete and land better jobs for more money and hence a "better and happier" life. The college admittance process has become a major source of pressure, stress and anxiety for students who are predominantly assessed on testing scores. The competition is fierce and the stakes high. Do we wonder why then most of our student body is medicated for some form of anxiety, depression, or ADHD? Instead of changing our way of life, we opt for medication so we can stay on the hamster wheel that we've now put into a pressure cooker to boot.

Our younger generation is suffering, and our adults are showing the strains and cracks of an unsustainable way of life. We are assessing and judging ourselves based on what we do and how we perform. We are basing our very value on our external achievements instead of who we are. Value is inherent, not acquired. We missed this important wisdom somewhere along the way causing marginalization of those who do not meet these extraordinary and unachievable standards. We are living a life that runs counter to our organic innate being. We are severely out of balance heading away from achieving and maintaining the very things we claim we desire. We make decisions and policies based on money and special interest and not what is for the greater good of human evolution. In short, the evolution of technology is far outpacing the evolution of human consciousness.

This trajectory needs to shift and return to a state of balance. Let's look at balance and the human identity.

CHAPTER 3

The Human Holy Trinity

We often hear the human existence referred to as three parts: mind, body, spirit.

As a society, especially Western society, we have focused on addressing and treating the "body". This is simply because it is the most tangible part of ourselves. Here we can control quite easily its well-being through the monitoring of diet and exercise. But we soon began to see that it wasn't a free-standing entity. We began to figure out that our mental state also played an important role in the optimal functioning of our body and its systems. We realized that there was a direct correlation between the mind and body, and science called this psychoneuroimmunology. We saw how common things like stress, anxiety, distress etc. affect the origins of illness and its manifestation in the body. As a result, research into this correlative state between mind and body took on a greater emphasis. How does our mental state affect what's happening in the body? What are thoughts? How are they formed? How do they affect our daily existence? The psychological community addressed all forms of mental distress and dis-ease with varying scientifically backed therapies, modalities, and medications. And yet, there still seemed to be a missing component.

This led us to the emotional body and the world of emotions, feelings, and belief systems. We began to correlate that our *experiences* affect and alter our emotions and feelings, which in turn affect our belief systems, which in turn affect our behavior. Most importantly, we began to perceive that these three things, the mind (mental), the body (physical) and the emotions were in fact "interconnected" as would be say a sophisticated bio-computer. We concluded that to have well-being all of these needed to work optimally and in conjunction with each other. The therapeutic community began to address these issues with multi-faceted approaches such as: EMDR, Somatic Therapy, EFT Tapping, IFS Therapy and the like. Yet, as needed, and as effective as they are, where is the missing component? Why is humanity still struggling despite all this assistance and knowledge? It's because we have put on the back burner and/or completely forgotten about the third aspect that makes up the trinity of our existence.

Anywhere you turn now, you see the term "inner work" and "turn within" being used as a resource to ascertain answers to our mental, emotional, and physical struggles. But what does that mean exactly? What does it mean when we say, "go within?" How do we enact it? And when we go within, what part of ourselves are we addressing? Who are we addressing, seeking to heal and get guidance from?

Inner work has to date has been referring to the modalities and therapies used to address the connection between the body, the mental and the emotional. However, inner work is primarily a spiritual process. Inner work *is* spiritual work and the third part of the human trifecta, and it plays much more of a significant role than we imagine.

So, why are we afraid to explore and address the spirit aspect of our being? What is it that makes this so complicated, so uncomfortable and so contentious? Perhaps because this aspect of our being is not physically tangible, but fluid in perception and needs to be explored without science and an instruction manual. We have mostly turned this aspect of ourselves over to religion; based on rules, dogma, and limitations, and to New Agers; presenting conflicting theories and distortions, and we are left with the impossible task of verifying what the truth is — something beyond what most of us want and can handle. In this manner we justify shutting down the whole process staying focused on the body and mind where we feel we have control and hence safety.

It is true that both religion and New Agers have distorted the truth for the benefit of personal agenda. Religions, although based on solid true spiritual foundations have historically distorted these truths in the name of power, greed, control, and ego. New Ager's have also distorted these truths in the name of greed, money, and ego. This leaves the masses with no way to discern what is authentic and what is distorted. As a result, some just stick to what they are born into, while others seek out New Age wisdom to explain the unexplainable, and still others have turned away from both and are living according to what they "believe to be true." They are "turning within" without realizing they are "turning within". They are by default following the organic process we all came into this life with. They are accessing their inner wisdom without giving it a name or a definition. They are for all intents and purposes **re-connecting** and accessing the spiritual part of themselves.

We see more and more people headed in this direction today than ever before. Everyone wishes to live the fullest expression of themselves, whatever that may be. However, most also believe they either have no idea how to do so or they feel blocked and don't understand why they can't get there. The answer is self-evident. Incorporating the spirit aspect of our being tangibly into our daily life, closes and brings into alignment the trinity of our being with spirit being the governing body, the origin, the compass of our human existence. Our mind and our body are created and designed to work in service to our spirit. The term "follow your heart" is a way we explain how we access our spiritual being.

Can you believe that you are a spiritual being having a temporary physical existence and not the other way around?

If we give credence to his truth, it shifts the very direction and manner with which we exist in our human lives. It predicates that our true home lies in a different form of existence which supersedes our human form of existence and is simultaneously all-wise, all-knowing, and omnipresent. This *is* our core identity and by learning to connect and understand it we develop a strong unshakeable sense of self that will weather all human struggle and conflict and eliminate fear in its most fundamental state.

Hence, here we have the human trinity – mind, body, spirit – that needs to stay in balance and alignment for optimal well-being. When one piece is out of sync, we become fragmented; giving away parts of ourselves to others and to the things that reside outside of ourselves in the material world. When we do this, we are like a twisty road with many off shoot ramps. Our energy becomes scattered in many directions breaking off from the center running amok while trying to find its way back to its source. When our mind, body and spirit is centered in our being and in our source from where it derives its power and life force, it is akin to a smooth well-oiled machine wherein all the parts are exactly where they should be, doing what they should do efficiently, easily, and effortlessly.

CHAPTER 4

The Case for Spiritual Identity

Spirtuality does not come from religion. It comes from our Soul. Religion is a set of rules (dogma or doctrine), regulations and rituals created by humans, which were initially designed to help people spiritually - to keep them close to God and to their own divine spiritual self. Religions were originally based on true spiritual foundations, teachings and practices but unfortunately over time due to the human false ego that generated the desire for power, control and greed; religion became anamorphic, corrupt, abused and misused for political gain and agenda, divisive and the ultimate tool for power struggle. It turned the divine/human "relationship" into "worship" driven and controlled by the teaching and instigation of fear. It completely diminshed and rendered the innate divine wisdom and intuition within each human being as untrustworthy thus creating co-dependency between religion and man. This is neither enlightening nor expansive, on the contrary it teaches people to kowtow, to see themselves as innately broken and imperfect, constantly repenting and worshipping. This type of theology alone creates the vices people act out because they are constantly looking for a redemption that never arrives (like a dangling carrot) so they choose to remain and engage, even revel, in the vices thinking it's a "no win win" anyway. This is how religion based on an underlying paradigm of fear and mercy remains in perpetuation.

Spirituality is not idealogy or theology or New Age, it is pure and authentic, it is **who you are** and a way of life that reflects your highest divine self. It is not worship, it is a relationship with the divine and your divine self. It is the network link to divine source, the universe and to each other. It is the origin and practice of unconditional love as defined by spirit; as the life force of the universe and everything in it. This love begins with full acceptance and love of the self, with the acknowledgement and understanding of your true identity. From this perception and knowing everything in your life shifts. It is not an intellectual concept to grasp from the external but rather reached from within. It is internal work that begins with opening to the possibility that you are much more than you have been led to believe, rendering hope to hopeless situations. It's a different standpoint that allows for self-empowerment, growth, progress, missteps and growth again. It allows for learning and evolution without self-annihilation and most of all with compassion, empathy and love for all existence – human and natural world. It breeds freedom on its most divine level and elevation out of the human ego constructs. And of course, unconditional love. This is the teaching and how its designed to be. This is the beginning of understanding our own sovereignty and the next step in our evolution.

CHAPTER 5

Labeling and the Notion of Separation

Humanity uses labels for everything. This is out of a need to classify information for easy assimilation and used to understand similarities and differences in culture, personalities, and basic human needs. This is not a negative technique but rather can be **used** negatively to cause stereotyping, expectations, judgements, prejudices, and subsequent trauma resulting in this feeling of separation from each other – this concept of "I'm over here and you're over there". This causes a two-fold problem within humanity.

First, we begin treating each other based on our labeling and social conditioning, teaching our children to do the same. The result is the perpetuation of a never-ending cycle of assumptions and judgements that in essence do not exist and drastically minimizes the hope of any course correction. Second, labeling causes a short circuiting, if you will, between who we think we are supposed to be and who we genuinely are, generating a constant internal conflict that causes an identity crisis.

In labeling we assign a group of characteristics to people (personalities and genders) and cultures, without the nuance of individuality, which focuses more on our differences than our commonalities. As such it has created stereotypes which have proved detrimental primarily in causing us to believe that we are a "separate species" from each other simply because we have diverse race, cultures, ethnicities etc. We have then used this notion of separation to condemn each other and engage in self-righteous behavior which has led to all manner of conflict both on the collective scale and in our personal lives.

When we engage in the judgement of another based on our external separating factors, we are attempting to validate ourselves as "better" so we may feel significant in some way. Why do we feel the need to do this? Why would we only feel significant and worthy if we condemn our fellow human as insignificant and unworthy? Why are we lacking a solid sense of self that would preclude such thinking?

Can we embrace the notion that our very diversity is by divine design? That it's the teaching and prompt for us to seek out, acknowledge and live by our common threads instead of ripping each other apart? That observing, experiencing, and integrating our polarities, leads to understanding, harmony and unification based on our common threads and our human origin as the purpose, the lesson, and the way forward?

To the second point, labeling instigates this inner conflict between who we think we are supposed to be and who we are. There is an internalization process labeling causes in the human psyche leading to a disconnection within, which then spills over into our self-perception. When we are strapped with labels, especially from a young age, we begin to accept and identify with them presuming this is who we are. This gradual process of believing our labels becomes our identity and we subconsciously begin to act or behave from this assigned label. The conflict arises when we start to realize we are not our label, and it does not express who we are. This then drives us to ascertain and examine who we genuinely are and what we believe as garnered from our own experiences and assessments and not what someone else handed to us or told us we were. This revelation spurs a soul-searching journey into our *authentic identity*. Everyone without exception begins this search externally, through our relationships, career, and life choices. Conducted consciously this will take us by default to our inner search. For the external search will glean only so much information about who we are. It will provide us with a portrait of our human upbringing and all it facets - an overall view of our human life with all its components. This is initially essential, for this data will assist us in re-defining our choices moving forward from the human perspective. However, at some point during our self-development the need to look deeper within will present itself. As we do this, we will begin to also understand our fellow humans and the common cords that bind us. So how do we process all this data? What mainframe do we put it through to help us reach our conclusions?

If you said the mind, you are only partially correct. The mind receives and inputs the data, but it is your spiritual being that guides your processing and conclusion. It is within your spiritual identity that all this data is integrated, most of us are just not consciously aware of it. Our spiritual identity is at work 24/7 pushing and prodding us until we recognize its existence and truth in directing our lives.

Another effect of labeling and the notion of separation it creates, is that we have assigned this mode of thinking to our concept of divine source and our divine self. We perceive ourselves as separate from our divine source. We have been conditioned to believe we are less than and therefore must remain in a constant state of proving ourselves worthy and good enough to extrapolate some sort of favor for an easy, abundant, happy life. In believing ourselves separate from divine source we do not utilize it or understand its teachings.

Furthermore, this concept of separation has been applied directly to divine source stating if humans are separate from each other then so are their divine source counterparts. Thus, we create divinity in our own image and ascribe to it humanity's attributes...anger, vengeance, jealousy, evil, nepotism, narcissism etc. Wars have begun and have been viciously fought over whose divine source and subsequent way of life is the "right way" or "only way" causing more separation and polarity. Again, we have not understood this polarity and what it is designed to teach us.

This separation theology we have constructed in all its forms exists because we have yet to perceive our true core identity. We have created divine source based on our own image and perceptions; rooted in separation to further justify and validate our separation from each other as opposed to witnessing and comprehending what our divine source genuinely is. We have struggled to access divine source and our inner identity mistakenly through our outer existence and our differences, wondering why there is so much conflict. We seek to discover purpose and vision and give meaning to our life individually and collectively from our external world when these answers can only come from our internal world.

Can we embrace the truth that there is no separation between us, our divine source and between each other? Can we love and cohabitate with each other without annihilating one another?

There is one divine source for all humanity, and we find that source when we learn and decide to turn within where it resides, to learn from where our inner compass, wisdom, and intuition stem from.

CHAPTER 6

Labels, Stereotypes and
Disconnection from the Self

Let's take a closer look at how labeling and stereotyping has caused a disconnection and internal conflict within us, between who we think we are supposed to be and who we genuinely are and how it has served to practically eradicate our sense of self.

Labeling has become this notion that everyone under a specific label live the same way with a list of expectations and a code of behavior – when there is agreement on this within the group/label everyone "feels" better – they feel as if they are doing something "right" because the whole group is following suit. This gives a feeling of security, safety and belonging - except when someone decides not to adhere to the specific code of behavior. That person is then labeled "bad and wrong" and in many cases demeaned and ostracized from the group. Stereotyping does not allow for individuality of thought and a cross sectioning of existence. It creates an all or nothing mentality and induces judgment in the most destructive ways. Groups/labels can be defined as religious, ethnic, business, political and social for the most part. Groups host several spoken and unspoken codes of behavior that are deemed appropriate and acceptable. When a new thought process is ventured forth by an individual than runs counter to the group, the common received commentary is "that's not how we do things" "you don't understand how life works, you haven't learned yet or you're confused, you should stop listening to other people" or "he/she is not like us". The individual then feels isolated for some of their different theories. This is because in a group any different thought process can be seen as a threat to the whole and the group is interested in self-preservation. Conformity at all costs is key to the group survival.

I witnessed across cultures that many people, to meet the expectations of the group/label they were born into, for the sake of belonging and believing "this is the way it is", modified their behavior accordingly much to the detriment of their individual critical thinking and authenticity. They followed along and behaved in ways that do not necessarily represent and coincide with their own innate nature, wisdom or expression. Eventually their inner voice becomes drowned out completely as they are too focused on trying to "fit in" or "do the right thing" for the sake of remaining accepted and acknowledged as defined by someone else. Is there any wonder we have so much unrest and masses of people moving away from anything that defines them in a limiting manner?

When an individual decides to march to their own drumbeat within the label they have been issued, everyone else in the group it seems conspires to take them down, to change their mind, to teach them how they have strayed away from the group's code of living. The perceived threat serves to de-legitimize and makes the remaining members feel inadequate. It exposes their own lack of courage, individual understanding, and fear of evolution beyond their label. They can act out on this with ostracization or even violence as emotions of resentment and jealousy are triggered.

As a result, the process of discerning whether the group or label you belong to represents who you are can be challenging and fraught with anxiety, stress, depression, insecurity, isolation, rejection, abandonment, and a sense of confusion. As you ascertain your own truths and beliefs, questioning and moving away from the beliefs you were handed you experience an internal conflict until you solidify what is aligned with who you are. During this process we experience our inner conflict as a sense of disconnection from our sense of self and our authenticity vs. what we were taught. We experience a variety of emotions; confusion, frustration, anger, pain from rejection, and conversely, we also experience joy, elation, relief, and liberation when we finally accept who we are without reservation, shame, or guilt.

The negative emotions can run rampant and cause havoc if they are not perceived within the context of your "personal growth." The internalization of these emotions can cause trauma when not released and understood for what they are. Remember, you are discerning what is true *for you*. This is your spiritual evolution as you continue to expand your identity through your experiences. You can do this without demeaning, insulting, or quarreling with the other members of the group, nor make them out to be "bad and wrong" despite how they might be treating you and your beliefs. This is not a case of right vs. wrong but rather what works or doesn't work for each person. Everyone is at a different stage in their spiritual, personal evolutionary self-development and may not yet be ready to question the status quo of society and where they reside in such. Respecting where everyone is at without judgement while finding your own authenticity is what continues to foster harmony.

The key is this: ask yourself: has everything you have come to believe about yourself, and life been taught to you by someone else? Where have you made your own discernments? Assessments? Reflect on this. Pull apart your belief system and question all of it. What still rings true – keep. What does not – discard with love and gratitude for what it taught you. Ultimately, only you know what serves you. If the label you have donned, along with those in your life who share them, do not accept, or support any differentiation on your part, then it's time to move on. You have simply outgrown them. Your consciousness has expanded, and you are evolving spiritually and emotionally. Let go with peace and love, do not make anyone else bad or wrong and move forward.

The Dangers of Labeling our Children

A word to parents/caregivers here: saddling our children with labels such as: fat/skinny, smart/average, lazy/disciplined, good looking/average, well-behaved/disruptive, etc. and my favorite; good/bad serves to undermine their own perception of who they are. Labeling children creates the foundation of their self-perception based on how **you** see them as opposed to allowing them to organically discover themselves. When you're labeling them in any way, positively or negatively, it becomes an internalized message that they will reflect back to you.

This is does not mean you cannot express love and affection, guidance, and regulation. It means you do so without the labels they will spend the rest of their life trying to unload. I have seen countless students in my practice from all walks of the socioeconomic spectrum and within their own relative existence battling some form of perception and expectation their parents/caregivers have of them that they can't and often don't want to live up to.

When I consult with the parents on this they are usually stunned, offended, defensive and in denial that their children even have a right to feel this way.

Here's what we need to know, children are our faithful mirrors. They observe and internalize our words and behaviors and reflect them back to us. This makes most parents uncomfortable, resistant, or angry especially when they are not flattering. The child hit a nerve without even realizing they were doing so. What an incredible teachable moment for the parent. Their beloved child is giving them the opportunity to notice, remember and acknowledge a wounded part of themselves they have disowned so it may be healed and released. This is not a form of some type of insubordination but a subconscious gift they give you to heal yourself by examining your own childhood labels and returning to your own truth. Everyone benefits when we see these moments and challenges from this perspective.

Children are spiritual beings of equal value to the adults around them. When we begin to understand and see **ourselves** as spiritual beings, engaged in the process of discernment and evolution we will then see our children this way as well. And as such, we will no longer see them as extensions of our egos or as some form of ownership. When we see them as mutual spiritual beings, that come in together with us as family, then our behavior will naturally and automatically reflect that belief and we will think twice or refrain from following human societal conventions of labeling, stereotyping, and judging. Give them the freedom to figure out who they are with you as their guiding force even if it wasn't given to you as a child. Be the adult who breaks this chain. Children are a wonderful gift. They remind us of who we once were and who we are presently by their sheer presence: our divine self, not our human self. This is why they are our "faithful mirrors".

One very special note on the children who come into the human existence with a desire to express a disability or special need. They are very special gifts, as they emphatically remind all of us of who we are spiritually at our core, and they serve to give us the opportunity to expand and stretch our love and compassion much beyond the current standard human convention. They give us the opportunity to see beyond the human physical and mental limitation, to see directly into the spirit and soul…directly into the love of our divine source. They serve as a spiritual bridge to humanity for the next stage of our evolution and for what is possible when we access our innate existence. No-where is it plainer to see than in these beings that have chosen this path. What a wonderful tribute they are to all they touch. They give us new definitions and parameters of the term unconditional love. They mirror back to us so clearly who we are. Is it any wonder in this time of great global chaos; politically, economically, environmentally, socially that we are seeing so many more of these beings being born? They are a testament everywhere to the love they bring and the opportunity for all of us to see that love reflected to us from their eyes.

Stereotypes and Disconnection

Of the many pitfalls of labeling is the creation of stereotypes. Ask anyone who has been stereotyped and they will tell you they seem to stick like glue for all eternity. Stereotypes are based on assumptions and lead to behavioral expectations and prejudices. Stereotyping runs rampant in our society today as never before simply because we are in ignorance, fear and polarized as never before. The exercise of stereotyping is external identification at its worst. It is solely based on our human existence without any awareness of or regard for our internal being. Its generalizations block our ability to observe and discern. It keeps us locked into a narrow perception of others that robs us of the richness of individuality and receptiveness of our differentiation.

When someone is at the effect of being perceived and judged via a stereotype, especially by someone they care for, it is hurtful, damaging, and traumatic. Chronic stereotyping at any level and in any area causes stress, anxiety, and a gradual disconnection from our sense of self. This disconnection results in low-self-esteem, negative self-image and self-perception, lack of motivation, inhibits clarity and serves as an overall stumbling block to personal growth. It causes us to lose our inner compass, question our identity and doubt all the qualities that constitute the fabric of our being. Our sense of self is eroded, stripped away from us by others who cannot acknowledge or accept that which is different from them. Being stereotyped invokes a thought process which says: "there is something innately wrong with me". We doubt, deny, and distrust our own existence often leading to a downward spiraling plagued with feelings of "not being good enough" and begin acting out or behaving in ways that reflect this belief. In short, we have an identity crisis.

It is at this juncture, between the labels, stereotyping, expectations, and judgements that we begin to question our existence, and purpose. The inward journey of healing and re-connecting to our truth begins here and it is in our spiritual identity where we will find the respite, fortitude, and truth we seek.

CHAPTER 7

Identifying as a Spiritual Being in a Human World

When we are born, we come into a specific race, gender, culture, ethnicity, geographical location, socioeconomic stratum, and parent/family psychological type. There are no accidents or coincidences. You incarnated for a reason and a purpose. Most of us know this as the internet is flooded with books and sites and guides on how to find your life's purpose.

On a grander scale and as a collective we are all here for the same shared purpose. We are here living our individual human lives gathering knowledge and insight through our experiences for the purpose of remembering who we are, spiritual beings of love. We are here to grasp this remembering with each experience, each relationship, each wound, each teaching, each lesson, and integrate it into our evolving life. Some of these experiences will be joyous and fulfilling and some will be painful and difficult. The human life is a device or mechanism, if you will, for reinforcing this truth.

How and to what degree we arrive at this truth is our individual journey. We each have free will to choose our direction, how we redeem our time, whether we embody our life lessons, whether we take the high road or indulge in our vices; our free will cannot be violated. Our choices however are a definition and demonstration of who we are at any given moment. Life constantly presents us with many choices so we may continue to refine and hone our identity and growth. Do we possess honesty, loyalty, integrity, dignity, respect, self-love? And if we do or don't, how does that make us feel about ourselves within? Observing and examining your choices is key to shifting.

Our choices stem from our belief systems. Our initial belief systems come from our nuclear family and immediate socioeconomic community. Our parents/caregivers pass down "a story" of who you are based on your race, culture, ethnicity. They also pass down gender roles and dynamics, and behavioral codes as to what is and isn't acceptable. Furthermore, if there is trauma, ancestral and family pain, repressed emotions, addictions and abuse they will pass this down as well in the form of non-verbal cues. All these components formulate our human identity. As children we pick up more from the actions and behavior of those around us than from what is being said. We internalize all the messages we receive, and it influences our personality, composes our inner dialogue - our "self-talk"- as well as our coping and defense mechanisms. It creates our self-perception. For example, if you are being raised by a narcissistic parent, you might cope by seeking validation from others forming co-dependent adult relationships.

Your self-talk will reflect low self-esteem, self-doubt and blame, indecision, lack of self-trust, and people pleasing tendencies, and this will become your self-perception. Monitoring your inner dialogue (self-talk) is the most useful tool you can use to trace back, examine and uncover where, what, and how your belief systems are shaping your future life.

Our personalities are mostly formatted in these early years and as we grow up, our social circle expanding, we play out the interactions of our childhood dynamics in real time. Coming into interaction with others is the defining way in which we learn about ourselves. How we relate to each other whether through friendship, as a colleague or romantic affiliation, relationships are our greatest teachers. The mirroring effect, discussed in Chapter 6 with children, is ever more present in our adult relationships. The purpose of relationships is to reflect the parts of ourselves and our upbringing, that we have repressed, denied, and disowned. When we are irritated or in conflict with someone it is because they have touched upon an aspect of ourselves we do not wish to see or acknowledge. To avoid this, we play the blame game and self-project, but this only ultimately serves in keeping us locked into victimhood. Victimhood does not allow for growth and gives this "stuck" feeling rendering us powerless. This is false, we are not powerless. We only feel this way because we are afraid to take ownership of our shadows and behaviors that bring up pain. Do not be afraid to practice radical honesty with yourself. Do not be afraid to look at the lesser aspects of yourself. By bringing it all up to the surface and out into the light, it can be healed and released. Remember you are a product of your social conditioning, it's not who you are. This knowledge is your superpower; social conditioning can be altered through the inner work of awareness, conscious choice, and tenacity thereof.

All our conflicts, difficulties, obstacles, and challenges can never be resolved at the level they were created, i.e., the human level. Solutions are found in a higher level of consciousness. When we face adverse situations where we feel we have exhausted every other means and reach a point of surrender we turn to divine source in supplication for a solution. But what if you knew you were already a primary component of that higher consciousness, divine source? How would that change your course of action and belief system? How would that change the way you address and move through life and its entire trajectory? You would still have challenges, but you would move through them completely differently. There would be an ease and less emotional triggering of situations where you might feel stuck, hopeless, at your wits end, or no way out. You would embrace obstacles as teachers and not as a condemning statement of who you **think** you are or supposed to be, as defined by another. You would fear less because you'll know you're inherently emotionally safe despite your challenges. This is the shift that takes place when you operate from the knowledge that your origin is spiritual in nature and your humanness is akin to a heavy costume you put on to experience your evolution experientially and by free will choice.

Your spiritual self is not a destination or a place, it's a state of being operating at a higher frequency. You have access to that frequency because you are that frequency as well. Imagine you came into this world wearing that very heavy coat over your body and you spend your lifetime removing it piece by piece. Your coat is made up of judgements, prejudices, fears, insecurities, doubts, etc. You are learning in this lifetime how to take off your coat to reveal and live as your "lighter" and "lighted" self.

When you realize and begin to live from the perspective of your spiritual being you won't take anything to heart because you're aware that everyone else is here working out their own lessons as well. You'll be able to maintain a more neutral stance in life and learn to observe and discern as a witness as opposed to judging and criticizing. You'll realize every experience is a teaching. You'll realize you are not your human story or your upbringing but that it is a vehicle of an experiential teaching to get you to the next step; to liberate you from all the negative labels, stereotypes, judgements, and criticisms and to cease utilizing them on others. You will realize you exist on another level as well and you will gravitate more and more to that space. You will begin to experience a level of liberation completely different than the human liberation. This is a liberation of the emotional shackles of your very existence.

Here is where your individual purpose will arise stemming from what you learned and if you share it, coupled with your innate gifts and talents, you can actualize being the change you wish to see in the world and your best self.

CHAPTER 8

Working in Tandem with our Spiritual Identity

We do not embody without carrying tools from our spiritual home with us. We are never left alone in this lifetime without guidance and direction. We have a spiritual team that works alongside of us. Unfortunately, though, not many are aware of this. We are aware however, that when a loved one dies, they send messages to us from the "other side" to let us know they are ok and watching over us. This is an initial understanding of our existence beyond the human life. This realization breeds the accompaniment of the thought that if they are watching over us, we can continue our relationship differently and they can guide us forward. This is true, they can and do so, in the form of signs sent via song lyrics, books, a conversation from a random stranger, etc. They will assist us in learning the lessons for which we have come. What they will not do is act as a short-order fairy godmother providing you with every desired materialistic toy. Rather, they will assist you in reaching your personal evolution mapped out for this current lifetime.

Our spirit guide team is tasked with this very goal, guiding your personal evolution. The many lessons we may have incarnated to experience and embrace singularly or in tandem could be tenacity, forgiveness, patience, higher learning, compassion, empathy, persistence, humility, inclusiveness, generosity and sharing, perseverance, leadership, teaching etc. As we experience our lives which ones apply will become self-evident. It is our job to recognize it and get to work learning and applying.

Along with our spirit guide team, we have other tools within us to use for communicating and working with them and our own spiritual self. It's important to note here that spirit, operating at a higher frequency will not appear or communicate in the human manner we are accustomed to. We must learn a new language if you will, the language of the unseen. Every method listed below requires a pre-requisite of setting aside our human false ego and its tendency to take over and run the show. We must quiet our humanness, meaning no outer distractions, no mind chatter, and no pre-conceived expectations.

How many times have you heard "get quiet", "sit in the stillness", "be silent"? This is because it is in the stillness and quiet and utter silence where you will hear spirit and your own spiritual voice. It will come as a nuance, a feeling and a knowing. We have come to call this *meditation*. This silence can be used as a two-way street. You can set an intention for your "dialogue" and converse silently through your mind or outwardly with your voice and then sit quietly for a length of time to allow and feel. Sometimes you will feel nothing, remember it takes patience and consistency. You don't become fluent overnight. For those who cannot "sit in meditation" note that meditation can occur when we are completely and wholly zoned into a task. This is because we are 100% absorbed in what we are doing on autopilot allowing the mind to get quiet. This can occur when we are absorbed in a craft, art, dance, or music. Also, gardening, cooking, ironing, or cleaning, doing a jigsaw puzzle, walking/running/swimming or other solo sport. There is no "one" way or "right" way. Use whatever resonates with you. The goal is to silence to the mind chatter so that you may hear your "spiritual voice".

Automatic writing is another method in which we can write out questions and then write the responses we receive. Many people do this by writing the responses received in their non-dominant hand to impede any interference on our part in controlling it.

Intuition and the language of feelings is still another; wherein you learn to become acutely aware of your feelings at any given time and the messages they send you. Listen to your nudges, which come as feelings, and then sit quietly to see what they are telling you. Your body is a great indicator here of what is being felt (for e.g. butterflies in your stomach expressing nervousness), given you have become adept at reading your body's responses in certain situations. This skill, although innate, requires your learning curve through awareness to decipher what your feelings indicate.

Dreams are very often vehicles used for the transference of messages. Learning to understand them as related to you specifically is key. Dream meanings are *not* generic. Symbols in dreams may have a universal meaning but how they apply to you specifically is unique to you and your life. Keep a journal by your bed and write them down as soon as you awaken, so you may go back and reflect on their meaning because once you get going with your day they may be forgotten.

Practicing gratitude in the spiritual sense, makes our inner world more tangible leading to greater self-acceptance and self-love. This means focusing on the non-tangible aspects of your being. Be grateful for insight, connection, wisdom, your breath, love, discernment etc.

Forgiveness is emotional liberation, and it *"allows"*. It assists us in ceasing self-punishment and punishment of another. It dissolves harbored guilt and shame, acknowledges errors, and ***allows*** for the space of course correcting without further self-sabotage.

Visioning in the spiritual sense is a tool that can be used to create intention and our next steps for our continued evolution.

Sitting in nature whether in a forest, on a beach or in the mountains is conducive to connection and stillness. The essence of the natural world with all its vastness presents a larger presence and perspective giving us clarity. It teaches us to look at the big picture hence calming our mind and minimizing any exaggerated sense of what appears as an insurmountable problem.

Animals with their loyalty, simplicity and unconditional love teach us what it means to just "be" and to connect without language. Spending time with them allows us to tap into these aspects of ourselves.

Breath Work is a whole-body exercise which alters our breathing patterns so we may learn to breathe with conscious awareness and intention to promote self-healing. It works in tandem with meditation. Our breath is our life-force and can be directed to serve us when consciously used for this purpose.

Observation and Discernment, my favorite tool. Observing from a neutral standpoint and discerning a situation allows for clarity of action, if any should be taken.

Observation allows you to step into the role of the witness which is free from any emotional charge which instigates judgement. Discernment allows for evaluation, assessment, and decision-making without said judgement. It allows for what does and does not reverberate within your being to present itself without criticism. I have come to learn that discernment comes from deep within our heart, from our spiritual self.

Past Life Regression conducted by a professional is a mild form of hypnotherapy which connects us with our past lives for the purpose of understanding your lessons in this lifetime. This modality can assist us in releasing and healing emotional traumas embedded in our system.

Self-Love is the epitome of the highest spiritual teaching. It does not derive from ego or as an intellectual exercise. It is the full acceptance of yourself; the good, bad and the ugly without judgement, criticism, or diminishment.

As I was writing this, I received a nudge to explain it in this way:

> *Embrace where you are right now in this moment on your journey. Do not judge it. Accept it, for it is your truth, at the moment, knowing that this truth is ever-expanding, as it should be. Do not be afraid to expand beyond what you currently know. Your current state is temporary until you move into your next stage of awareness, awakening and understanding.*
>
> *Know that you are light…your core is made up of light…there is no one on this planet who does not have this light. What you see is the degree and awareness each of us has of this light. There are many who are still in the denser stages of unawareness and ego and their light is much dimmer, but it is there and therefore, there is always hope and possibility to expand this light*

should they desire and chose it and become aware of it. The more aware, the further the pull to expand it. For that light is home and as it expands you will resonate more and more with those who match your light quota and frequency. Shifts in circumstances, because of your expanding light, is not bad or wrong, refrain from judging everything in these terms. Recognizing truth and light in another will be evident by your inner knowing.

CHAPTER 9

The Spirit/Matter Duality
and Creating Balance

You might have often read or come across literature that discusses our dual existence, referring respectively and accurately to the spirit world and the human world (also known as the world of matter or physicality). We experience this duality in our daily lives as a push/pull presence. Our work is to create a balance within our human state, by aligning our mind, body, and spirit and to then create balance and integration of our human state with our divine self and divine source. This is not as challenging as it sounds as in essence it's all interconnected. We cannot bring our human trinity (Chapter 3) into its internal alignment without our divine self and source coming into balance with it. It's one process and can be fraught with challenges when we are unaware of the internal dynamics.

Understanding the Role of Ego

Our human world is also referred to as the world of ego. When it comes to understanding the ego, I like to break it down and simplify things for clarity. I break it down as such: true self, ego, and false ego. Our true self is our eternal spiritual being, the epicenter and total sum of everything we are. Our ego is our existence as a unique individual human being aware of both our identities and acting as our gatekeeper. Our false ego is when we identify only with our human body and material existence. It's based on the one-dimensional concept we create about ourselves during our lifetime. It contains our shadow side and lies hidden just beneath the ego.

The ego is the crossroad between our true self and the false ego. It resides in our mind and can be healthy, serving the true self or unhealthy, serving the false ego. This is the push/pull presence mentioned above. The ego is in a constant state of calibrating which state to follow: the true self or false ego. This is where we activate our free will choices. What will we choose in any given moment? Which is stronger and directing our life?

All of us, without exception, knows how this dynamic plays out in our lives. Our false ego with its inaccurate composite of the self, derived from our woundings, traumas and emotional damage will continue to self-sabotage our life via repeated destructive patterns until we take notice and begin to unravel what is happening. The process of digging out these shadowed wounds is to heal and release them so balance may be restored. The patterns may include the running amok of negative behaviors (greed, jealousy, pride, resentment, selfishness etc.), a self-appointed grandiosity and prestige, constant need for adoration to name a few. When allowed to run wild for too long, we will eventually believe the false tale it tells us about ourselves, our idealized self-image. It will steer us far from our true self down into a rabbit hole of self-destruction if we do not pay attention and re-calibrate.

Our true self/spiritual self on the other hand, allows for the exploration and fullest expression of who we are. It exists in the stillness as we mentioned and is always present. It will always call out the false ego with its behaviors and actions for the purpose of healing and restoring balance to the human life. It will show us the way in increments and influence the ego by a constant steady building of the spiritual inner light. This light weakens the false tale the false ego likes to tell bringing healing. It will also bring us into alignment within ourselves and our divine source simultaneously. It will continue to expand our consciousness, upgrade our choices, and restore our inner state to one of peace and happiness.

Sound too good to be true? It isn't but we believe it is because unfortunately we have become so accustomed to living in a world replete with emotional drama, distrust, deception, selfishness, disrespect, lacking integrity etc. We, as a human collective, have let our false ego grab the reins and go. It's time we pulled those reins back to restore balance. We do this by making a conscious decision, at some point, (usually brought on by emotional crisis) to direct our ego to the path of serving and living through our spiritual being. In this way we can discover our authenticity living out our human lives from this narrative.

CHAPTER 10

———•◉•———

Tools from Home

Our spiritual home wishes to teach us that we are sovereign. It does this by giving us free will choice, which they never violate, and some guidelines. For this particular book, I have outlined them only. However, being sovereign from the spiritual perspective means "no head above your own". Only you know what is right for you and your human journey. It's been mapped out into your system before you incarnated. As helpful as someone else might be, and they can be, and as you read and learn from other sources, ultimately you discern for yourself what is right for you using the tools from spirit as your guide and the wisdom they impart. When in doubt turn within and seek out your answers. A response will always arrive. Stay open and mindful. This is the inner work.

Imagine your spirit team as your unseen partner and advisor assisting you in navigating your life. Lean into their messages and the vehicles they use to send them. Exercise humility and be open to learning, for a humble heart masters the lessons more effectively. The human identity is used to deepen the spiritual one. It's not one or the other, but rather an integration of both our existences with creating *balance* as the goal.

Connect. Connect. Connect.

The 12 Universal Laws

These are laws that are inherent and fundamental to the universe we live in. They are not created by humans but by spirit. They are immutable, always functioning and they describe how the universe works in this time space continuum. The Laws inter-relate as they are inter-connected. They are designed to work as a whole unit but are broken down individually to aid in understanding and developing mastery in increments one at a time.

Law of Divine Oneness

This is the first most important foundational law of the universe. It states that everything is connected to everything else. There is no separation. We are all one and all connected to source.

Law of Vibration

This Law states that everything in the universe is vibrating at a specific frequency. This includes all matter, as every particle vibrates. And applies to us too, as we all have a personal frequency.

Law of Correspondence

This Law states that our external circumstances and reality directly reflect our inner reality or state of being. As within, so without.

Law of Attraction

This Law states that like attracts like. You are attracting the same vibrational frequency you are at. This applies to everything.

Law of Inspired Action

This Law states that as a spiritual being connected to source, inspiration comes when you are in divine alignment, and you act on it. To achieve something, you must take inspired action and allow the universe to work for you.

Law of Perpetual Transmutation of Energy

This Law states that the universe is forever changing. The energy is in a constant state of evolution and fluctuation. Our own vibration is constantly fluctuating; for e.g., negative, or positive.

Law of Cause and Effect

This Law is also the Law of Karma. It is the direct link between action and reaction, thoughts, and experiences. It is a boomerang of what goes around, comes around.

Law of Compensation

This Law states the "reap what you sow" effect. It is about the quality of what you give and put out and is described as "you get as good as you give".

Law of Relativity

This Law states that everything is neutral, and we give it meaning based on our own perspective and perception creating relativity. Perspective is everything in our challenges.

Law of Polarity

This Law states that everything in the universe has an opposite, cold/hot, short/tall, love/fear.

Law of Rhythm

This Law states that the universe moves in natural cycles, like the four seasons. We move with the ebb and flow of life.

Law of Gender

This Law states that the divine masculine and divine feminine within each of us, is in balance and working harmoniously.

Final Thoughts

I wanted to leave you with this closing thought. An identity crisis is not a sign of anything innately wrong with you. If anything, it is an awakening for a new more authentic beginning. It is your education and re-education back into spiritual oneness with yourself, your source and with everyone else. It is in essence a solo journey within yourself.

You never have to feel alone, powerless, afraid and without guidance. You already carry within you as part of your spiritual identity all the tools you need to live the life you embody. It's time to learn a new language and to connect. Turn off all the outer distractions and spend more quiet time with yourself. You will laugh, you will cry, but eventually you will fall in love with yourself and from their all else begins anew.

Preamble on Book Two in the Human Case of Mistaken Identity Series

Self-Love: the Journey Home

The energy that moves the entire universe is love. Not the human definition of love, but the spiritual one and it begins with self-love. In my next book in this series, I explore the pathway to self-love as the utmost unifying route to emotional liberation, harmony, and evolution.

Self-love is the healing balm of your soul. It is the means that helps you release your emotional trauma and your pain. It is the way you feel safe and remove your emotional armor. It is the road to your forgotten heart and your childhood innocence. It is how you learn to honor yourself unconditionally and live your authenticity. It leads you to discovering your identity.

It is the journey back to yourself and to home.